HOW TO T
PEOPLE A`I WORK

The Ultimate Guide to How to Talk, Interact and Communicate With Difficult People with Challenging Personalities

Carina Whyte

TABLE OF CONTENTS

Practice active listening

Be present in the moment

Avoid giving advice

Be a good role model

5 REASONS WHY EMPATHY AT WORK IS A NECESSITY

Empathy allows you to see both sides of every issue

Empathy builds trust and rapport with colleagues

Empathy helps you understand different perspectives

Empathy allows you to resolve conflicts effectively

Empathy makes you a better leader

CONCLUSION

INTRODUCTION

In our everyday lives, it is inevitable that we will come in contact with difficult people at some point. Whether it's a co-worker, boss, or family member, there are certain people who just seem impossible to please. If you're struggling with how to deal with a difficult person in your life, you're not alone.

Are difficult people standing in the way of your success at work? Do you often find yourself feeling frustrated and overwhelmed when interacting with difficult personalities? The good news is that there are some tried and true strategies for dealing with difficult people.

From understanding their behaviour patterns to setting boundaries, you will learn how to navigate challenging situations and maintain a positive mindset.

There are different kinds of difficult people in the workplace, whether it's a difficult boss, coworker or client. You cannot change others or the way they talk and act, but you can control how you react and handle difficult situations. Difficult people can be found anywhere and everywhere and the workplace is no exception. Don't let difficult personalities hold you back from success.

Dealing with difficult personalities can be difficult, but with the strategies and steps in this guide, you will learn how to approach and interact with difficult people in a positive and professional manner.

Take control of difficult interactions and enhance your professional relationships. Start the journey towards confidently navigating difficult people today.

This guide will provide you with practical steps on how to effectively communicate with difficult people in the workplace.

CHAPTER 1

Why Are People Difficult?

There are many different ways to be difficult. Some people are difficult because they have a difficult personality. Others are difficult because of the way they were raised, or because of their experiences in life. And still, others are difficult because they simply do not know how to be any other way.

Difficult people often make life more difficult for those around them. They may be argumentative, inconsiderate, or just plain difficult to get along with. While some difficult people are simply born that way, others learn to be difficult as a result of their upbringing or life experiences.

So why exactly are people difficult? Here are some possible explanations:

They've had a Difficult Life

Some people are difficult because they've had a difficult life. They may have experienced abuse, trauma, or other difficult circumstances that have made them the way they are. As a result, they may be difficult to get along with because they're angry, resentful, or just plain difficult to please.

They Were Raised That Way

Some people are difficult because they were raised that way. Their parents may have been difficult people themselves, and they learned from their example. Or, their parents may have been too lenient, leading to spoiled and entitled children who never learned how to compromise or respect others.

They're Insecure

Many difficult people are actually quite insecure. They act out because they feel inadequate or unworthy. Deep down, they may feel like they're not good enough, so they try to compensate by being difficult.

They Want Attention

Some difficult people act out because they want attention. They may feel like they're not getting the attention they deserve, so they try to get it by being difficult. This is often a cry for help, as difficult people often feel neglected or misunderstood.

They Enjoy Causing Drama

Finally, some difficult people simply enjoy causing drama. They get a thrill out of stirring up trouble and making life difficult for those around them. This may be due to a mental disorder or just plain old-fashioned meanness.

Difficult people are a fact of life, but you don't have to let them ruin your life. With the right help, you can learn to deal with them in a way that works for you.

Chapter 2

Types of difficult people in the workplace

Working with difficult people can be challenging, but it's important to remember that everyone has their own quirks and personality traits. Just because someone is difficult to work with doesn't mean that they're a bad person. It just means that you have to find a way to work together that suits both of your needs. With a little patience and understanding, you can learn how to work with anyone - even the most difficult people.

The Know-It-All

This person is always quick to point out when someone else is wrong, and they love being the centre of attention. They can be difficult to work with because they often hog the conversation and don't listen to others' opinions. They want to be right all the time, even if it means trudging over others.

Always acknowledge the know-it-all and tell them that their idea is well appreciated. Also let them know your own solution and if they still push their idea down your throat tell them that you have made up your mind about using your own solution.

The Silent Type

They are the opposite of the know-it-all. They never speak up in meetings, they're difficult to read, and you always wonder what they're thinking. They can be frustrating to work with because it's hard to get gauge their opinion or get them involved in the conversation. They can go as far as plugging their ears with their ear phones all day just to shut out everybody or simply confine themselves to their cubicle.

However, some people think they are the best people to work with because they don't bother anybody, they are not involved in office gossip. They would rather want to be left alone in their own world.

If you really want to start a conversation with a quiet person then small talk should do the magic. It is advisable to rehearse what you are going to say to keep the conversation going.

The Pessimist

This person is always looking at the negative side of things. They're the Debbie Downer of the group, and they tend to bring everyone else down with them. It can be difficult to work with a pessimist because they're always seeing the glass as half empty instead of half full. Having a conversation with them is difficult because they're always bringing up negative points, no matter what the topic is.

The Optimist

This person is always looking at the positive side of things. They're the Pollyanna of the group, and they tend to make everyone else feel better with their optimistic outlook. Their positive attitude makes them more comfortable to work with but with caution.

The Drama Queen/King

They love to stir up drama and they're always at the centre of it. They love attention and they feed off of other people's reactions. It can be difficult to work with someone who's always causing drama because it's difficult to stay focused on the task at hand.

Drama queens are all about drama and you should not be seen to enjoy the drama. Spare no part of your day to interact with and tell them you are busy today.

Be sure not to buy into their perception otherwise you can be easily manipulated and become a drama queen yourself.

The Gossip

The gossip loves to talk about other people, and they're always up on the latest gossip. They love to spread rumours and they're always looking for juicy details. They are not easy to work with because it's difficult to trust them. You never know if they're going to say something negative about you behind your back.

If you really want to shut down the gossip mongers, whenever they come with a topic ask them for facts to back up what they are saying. When they know that you will ask for facts they will back down at a point.

It also helps if you don't give them a listening ear or just tell them you are not interested. You can also tell them you don't want to get involved in such talks.

The Negative Nelly/Nancy

This person is always seeing the glass as half empty instead of half full. They're pessimistic and they tend to bring everyone else down with them. It can be difficult to work with a negative person because they're always looking at the dark side of things. When having a conversation with them one is always on the defensive.

The Difficult Customer

This person is always demanding and they're never happy with what they get. They're always complaining and they're never satisfied. It can be stressful to work with a difficult customer because you always feel like you're falling short. No matter what you do, it's never good enough for them.

The Complainer

This person is always complaining about something. It could be the weather, their job, traffic, you name it. They're never happy and they love to complain about everything. No matter what you do you can never please them because they're always going to find something to complain about.

The Bully

Bullies love to pick on others and make them feel inferior. This can make them difficult to work with because they're always putting others down and making them feel bad about themselves. It is not easy to stand up to a bully, but it's important to do so. Otherwise, they'll continue to try and control you and make your work life difficult.

When dealing with bullies you need to speak up early so that the issue can be squashed before it escalates. Keep a record of any abuse so that there will be evidence when you finally report to your boss. This means that when all else fails you should report to your boss.

Chapter 3

Handling Difficult People in the Workplace: Tips for Success.

No two people are alike, and that's especially true in the workplace. You may have co-workers who are easy to get along with, and then there are those who just seem to rub you the wrong way. Maybe they're always critical, or they're constantly trying to one-up you. Whatever the case may be, difficult people can make going to work feel like a drag.

But they don't have to ruin your day. With a little bit of strategy and finesse, you can successfully navigate even the most challenging personalities. Here are some tips for doing just that:

How to Talk to a Difficult Boss

If you're having trouble with a difficult boss, there are a few things you can do to try to improve the situation. Stay professional and calm at all times. This can be difficult if your boss is constantly yelling or making demeaning comments, but you need to remain level-headed.

Try to build a rapport with your boss by engaging in small talk and showing an interest in his or her life outside of work.

In addition, be sure to document everything. This way, if your boss does say or do something that crosses the line, you have evidence to back up your claim.

Finally, don't be afraid to speak up for yourself. If your boss is being unfair or unreasonable, calmly state your case and explain why you think he or she is wrong. Some bosses can be difficult to deal with, but by following these tips, you can work around it.

How to Talk to Difficult Co-Workers

If you're having trouble with a difficult co-worker, there are a few things you can do to try to improve the situation. Try to engage in small talk and get to know your co-worker on a personal level.

Also, be understanding and patient if your co-worker is going through a tough time. We all have bad days, and sometimes people take that out on those around them.

Third, don't take things personally. If your co-worker is constantly criticizing you or putting you down, it's probably not about you.

Don't be afraid to set boundaries. If your co-worker is crossing the line, calmly explain what he or she is doing that is making you uncomfortable and ask him or her to stop.

How to Talk to Difficult Customers

When things are not going well with a difficult customer, there are a few things you can do to try to improve the situation. You need to stay professional and calm at all times. This can be difficult if the customer is being rude or insulting, remain polite and patient.

Try to see things from the customer's perspective. He or she may be having a bad day or may be dealing with something difficult in his or her personal life.

Be sure to apologize even if the problem isn't your fault. This shows that you're willing to take responsibility and that you're trying to make things right. Finally, offer a solution. If the customer is unhappy with a product or service, try to offer him or her a refund or an alternative option.

How to talk to difficult people in general

When you are not getting along with difficult person in general, especially outside the workplace, the same strategies often apply.

Stay calm and collected at all times. This can be difficult if the person is being rude or insulting, but remain polite and patient. Second, try to see things from the person's perspective. Assess the situation and don't be quick to act or react.

Applying these five tips can help you successfully navigate even the most difficult personalities. Remember, difficult people don't have to ruin your day. With a little bit of strategy and finesse, you can find ways to get along with even the most challenging personalities. So next time you're faced with a difficult person, take a deep breath and put these tips into practice. Good luck!

Chapter 4

Importance of Communication in the Workplace and Some Key Strategies for Success.

At work, communication is essential to building strong relationships with your colleagues and successfully accomplishing your goals. Whether you are leading a team or working as part of a larger group, effective communication is critical for achieving success.

By using these strategies and adapting them to your specific context, you can effectively influence others through effective communication and build strong relationships that help drive results.

In this chapter, we will explore some key communication strategies that can help you succeed in the workplace. These include listening actively, using clear language and expressions, staying open-minded and flexible, and communicating effectively across different platforms, such as email or meetings.

Listen actively

To start, it is important to listen actively when engaging with others at work. This means giving people your full attention when they are speaking and really taking in what they are saying, rather than simply waiting for your turn to talk. You can also ask clarifying questions or reflect on what you are hearing in order to gain a deeper understanding of the other person's point of view.

Use clear, simple language and expressions

This means avoiding jargon or technical terminology, as it can often get in the way of communication and make it difficult for others to understand what you are saying. Instead, try using plain language that is easily understandable, even if some colleagues might consider it "too simple."

Stay open-minded and flexible

This means being approachable, receptive to feedback and ideas from others, and willing to reconsider your own opinions if necessary.

Different platforms for communication

Communication in the workplace often involves interacting with people over different platforms, such as email or meetings. As such, it is essential to be aware of the communication style that works best for each platform. For example, when communicating via email, you may want to keep your messages short and simple, while in meetings you might use a more conversational tone to encourage active participation from others.

Effective communication in the workplace

Effective communication is essential for success in the workplace. Whether you are interacting with your colleagues, clients, or superiors, communication skills can have a major impact on your ability to get things done and achieve your goals. Some key examples of effective communication in the workplace include:

Building trust and rapport

Strong communication skills enable you to build trust and rapport with others, creating positive relationships that facilitate collaboration and help you get things done more quickly. This includes being open and honest in your interactions, listening actively to others' perspectives, and communicating clearly in order to avoid misunderstandings.

Establish common goals and objectives

Set clear expectations for what you hope to achieve and establish a shared understanding of how to move forward. Some strategies for establishing common goals and objectives include:

Defining your goals

This involves clearly articulating what you hope to accomplish, as well as the steps you will take to achieve those goals. By breaking down larger objectives into more manageable pieces, it is easier to set achievable targets and track progress along the way.

Setting timelines and deadlines

To help keep everyone on track, it is important to set realistic timelines and deadlines for meeting your goals. This can involve establishing regular communication checkpoints to keep everyone up-to-date on progress and adjust as needed.

Engaging others in the process

When it comes to achieving common goals, communication is a two-way street. To be successful, there is a need to get input from others and involve them in the decision-making process whenever possible. Whether this means collaborating with teammates, consulting clients or stakeholders, or seeking feedback from your manager, engaging others can help build consensus and encourage commitment to shared objectives. With the right communication strategy in place, you can establish common goals and objectives that will help drive success at work.

In most cases collaborating with your teammates is the best way of communication within the workplace. This can involve holding regular meetings to discuss progress, sharing feedback and ideas, or simply talking one-on-one with colleagues when you have questions or concerns. By communicating effectively and building strong relationships with your team mates, you can work together more productively and achieve great things in the workplace.

Close with a call to action

To close with a call to action, consider taking the following steps:

Be open to feedback and collaboration from others.

This can include seeking input from your manager or teammates, consulting clients or stakeholders, or simply engaging in dialogue with those around you.

Embrace change as an opportunity for growth.

In order to adapt to new challenges and opportunities, it is important to stay open-minded, receptive to feedback, and willing to try new things.

While being open to feedback is essential, ensure that some of the team's suggestions are implemented. This can help to build trust and respect among team members, and ultimately lead to greater success. Additionally, by embracing change and taking initiative in your communication efforts, you can achieve great things at work.

Chapter 5

Top 12 tactics for dealing with personality challenges

Difficult people are inevitable in any workplace. You know the type: they are always negative, they're constantly challenging you, and they make it their mission to make your life difficult. Their actions always result in unnecessary conflict.

Personality challenges are very likely to result in some form of unconducive atmosphere in the workplace.

How you deal with them, however, is entirely up to you. If you find yourself regularly struggling to manage difficult personalities, try out some of these tactics:

Establish clear boundaries

The first step to dealing with difficult people is to establish clear boundaries. Explain what behaviours are acceptable and what are not, and be consistent in your enforcement. This will help difficult people understand what they can and cannot get away with.

Communicate Assertively

When communicating with difficult people, it is important to be assertive. This means being clear, direct, and firm in your communication. Avoid using passive or aggressive communication styles, as they will only aggravate the situation.

Being direct is desirable as vague communication is one of the main reasons difficult situations spiral out of control. If you're clear and direct in your communication, there will be less room for miscommunication and misunderstanding.

Avoid Taking Things Personally

Difficult people often say and do things that are designed to get a reaction out of you. It is important to avoid taking these things personally, as doing so will only give the difficult person power over you.

Keep Your Emotions in Check

When you're dealing with a difficult person, it's important to remain level-headed. They can be very emotionally charged and difficult to deal with when you are also feeling emotional. Getting angry or emotional will only make it harder for you to communicate effectively and make it more likely that the situation will escalate.

Be Willing to Compromise

Difficult people are often inflexible and unwilling to compromise. However, if you are willing to meet them halfway, it can often help diffuse the situation.

Don't Stoop To Their Level

If a difficult person is constantly trying to goad you into an argument, don't take the bait. By responding in a calm and rational manner, you'll diffuse the situation and show that you're the better person.

Avoid Reacting Impulsively

Difficult people often try to bait you into reacting impulsively. It is important to avoid doing this, as it will only give them the satisfaction of knowing they got under your skin.

Don't Let Down Your Guard

Difficult people are often manipulative and can take advantage of you if you let your guard down. It is important to be aware of this and to not let down your guard, even for a moment.

Be Firm in Your Convictions

Difficult people will often try to convince you to change your mind or do things their way. It is important to be firm in your convictions and to stand up for what you believe in, even if it means being difficult yourself.

Seek support

Difficult people can make it difficult to cope with the situation on your own. If this is the case, seek support from your manager or Human Resources.

Find Common Ground

Another step is to find common ground. What do you have in common with a difficult person? What interests do you share? By finding common ground, you can build a rapport and start to work together.

Take a break

Finally, if all else fails, sometimes the best thing you can do is to take a break from the difficult person. This may mean avoiding them altogether or simply taking some time for yourself to recharge.

Chapter 6

Learn to Ask Questions

What Questions to Ask Difficult People in the Workplace

Asking questions is a great way to learn more about someone's point of view and find common ground. By taking the time to ask questions, you can improve your communication skills and make progress in your career.

Questions are asked to clarify, probe, or understand someone's perspective on a situation. Questions can also be used to build relationships.

When you're talking to difficult people in the workplace, it's important to ask questions in a respectful way. This shows that you're willing to listen to their point of view and try to see things from their perspective. Asking questions is a great way to learn more about someone's thoughts on a matter, and it can help you find common ground.

Here are some examples of questions you could ask difficult people in the workplace:

- How do you feel about the situation?

- What do you think is the best course of action?

- What are your thoughts on the matter?

- What can we do to resolve this issue?

- How can I help you?

By taking the time to ask questions, you can improve your communication skills and make progress in your career. Learning how to ask questions is a valuable skill that can help you in many aspects of your life.

Chapter 7

Small Talk Is In the Mix

Small talk is a social skill that may seem pointless, but it can actually be a helpful tool in the workplace. Though it is informal it is a way of building a foundation and filling in awkward moments when trying to form a relationship. Small talk can help you build relationships, learn about others, and make progress in your career.

How and When to Use Small Talk

So how and when should you use small talk in the workplace? Here are some tips:

Get to know your co-workers

Small talk is a great way to get to know your co-workers. When you're talking to someone, ask them questions about themselves and their interests. This is a great way to start building relationships.

Learn about others

Small talk can also be used to learn about others. By listening more than you talk, you can find out what the other person is interested in and what they're looking for in a job.

Make progress in your career

Small talk can also be used to make progress in your career. If you're talking to someone who is higher up in the company, ask them for advice or ask about opportunities that may be available.

By following these tips, you can learn how and when to use small talk in the workplace. So don't be afraid to start making small talk today!

Small talk topics

Sometimes small talk topics don't easily come to mind when you are dealing with a difficult situation but here are some small talk questions you can use to start a conversation when you need them, especially at work.

How are you coping with your new job role?

What was your last job like?

Why did you decide to work in this occupation?

It was quite snowy yesterday, how did you get home?

Is there anything you would like to add to your new office?

There are many things you can talk about depending on the situation you are handling. Sometimes starting small talk can be quite uncomfortable because you are trying to break the ice but with practice, you can become very skilled.

When starting out small talk conversations should be work-related and after establishing some rapport it can be extended to food, weather, or other trending issues. Just be creative and begin to use small talk as part of your communication skills.

It is possible that you have exhausted all your options and still nothing seems to have worked and there is no solution, ensure that you have documented all your actions and the outcome. Then it's time to report to your manager and Human Resources who might help find a solution.

Chapter 8

Empathy, the Communication Skill You Need Most

What is empathy and why do we need it in our lives?

Empathy is the ability to understand and share the feelings of another. It is a vital communication skill that we need in our lives, both personal and professional.

If you can learn to empathize with the difficult people around you, you'll find that it's much easier to get along with them. Empathy will help you to understand their perspective and to see things from their point of view. It will also make it easier for you to build rapport and trust.

Types of empathy

There are three main types of empathy: cognitive, emotional, and compassionate. All three types of empathy are important in our lives. They help us to build better relationships, to understand others better, and to create a more positive world.

Cognitive empathy

This is the most intellectual form of empathy. It's the ability to see things from another person's perspective and to understand their feelings. This type of empathy is important in our lives because it helps us to build better relationships. When we can see things from another person's perspective, we can better understand their needs and wants. We can also avoid misunderstandings and conflict.

Emotional empathy

This is the ability to feel another person's emotions. It's the ability to sense what they're feeling and to share in their emotional experience. This type of empathy is important in our lives because it helps us to build stronger relationships. When we can feel what another person is feeling, we can show them compassion and care. We can also better understand their needs and wants.

Compassionate empathy

This is the ability to care about another person's welfare. It is the desire to help them, even if there's nothing in it for you. This type of empathy is important in our lives because it helps us to create a more positive world. When we show compassion for others, we can inspire them to do the same. We can also make a difference in their lives by helping them when they need it most.

No matter what type of empathy you practice, it is important to remember that empathy is a two-way street. It's not just about understanding and caring for others, but also about being open to understanding and being cared for yourself. Empathy is an essential part of any healthy relationship.

Here are some tips on how to be more empathetic with the difficult people in your life:

Listen more than you talk

When you're talking to someone, really try to listen to what they're saying. Don't just wait for your turn to speak. Really pay attention to their words and their body language. This will help you to understand them better.

Put yourself in their shoes

Try to see things from the other person's perspective. Try to understand why they feel the way they do. This will help you to empathize with them more.

Avoid Judging Them

It is easy to judge people when we don't agree with them or when we don't understand them. But it is important to avoid judgment if we want to be empathetic. Try to see things from their point of view, even if you don't agree with it.

Be patient

Empathy takes time and patience. It's not something that you can do overnight. But the more you practice, the better you'll get at it.

Ask questions

If you're not sure about something, ask the other person about it. This will help you to understand them better and to build rapport.

Try To Understand the Other Person and You Will Be Understood In Return

This is one of the strongest pillars of empathy. Seek first to understand the other person, before trying to make them understand you. This will help you to connect with them on a deeper level.

Practice active listening

Active listening is a communication technique that involves really paying attention to the other person, paraphrasing what they say, and asking questions. It's a great way to show empathy and to build rapport.

Be present in the moment

When you're talking to someone, really focus on them and on the conversation. Don't let your mind wander. This can be difficult, but it's important if you want to be truly empathetic.

Avoid giving advice

It is not always helpful to give advice, even if you think you know what's best for the other person. Sometimes, people just need to be heard and understood. So instead of giving advice, just listen and try to understand.

Be a good role model

If you want others to be more empathetic, you need to be a good role model yourself. Practice empathy in your own life, and encourage others to do the same.

5 Reasons Why Empathy at Work Is a Necessity

Empathy is one of the most important qualities you can possess in the workplace. It allows you to see both sides of every issue, build trust and rapport with colleagues, and resolve conflict effectively. Here are 5 reasons empathy at work is a necessity:

Empathy allows you to see both sides of every issue

If you can understand where someone is coming from, it's much easier to find common ground and resolve conflicts. Empathy also allows you to have more productive conversations, as you're more likely to understand the other person's point of view.

Empathy builds trust and rapport with colleagues

If your colleagues feel like you understand them and their concerns, they're more likely to trust and respect you. This is especially important in team environments, where trust is essential for effective collaboration.

Empathy helps you understand different perspectives

In a workplace, there are often many different voices and opinions. Empathy allows you to see all sides of an issue and come to a better understanding of the situation. This can help prevent misunderstandings and miscommunication.

Empathy allows you to resolve conflicts effectively

Conflict is inevitable in any workplace. However, empathy can help you resolve conflicts faster and more effectively. When you understand where the other person is coming from, it's easier to find a compromise that everyone can agree on.

Empathy makes you a better leader

Leaders need to be able to see things from multiple perspectives and empathize with their team members. Empathy allows you to build trust, inspire others, and make better decisions for your team. If you want to be a successful leader, empathy is a necessity.

CONCLUSION

When faced with difficult people in the workplace, it is important to remember that communication is key. By staying calm and keeping an open mind, you will be better equipped to handle the situation. If you find yourself getting upset, take a step back and try to see the situation from the other person's perspective.

It can also be helpful to role-play difficult conversations with a friend or colleague before facing the person in question. Finally, always be willing to compromise and look for common ground. By following these tips, you can turn difficult conversations into productive ones.

Finally, being able to show empathy helps you to be a better leader who understands people for who they are and is able to handle difficult people because he has built trust and rapport in the work environment.

Applying your communication skills in difficult situations will not only make work life easier but can also help to build better relationships with the people you work with.

Printed in Great Britain
by Amazon